COSMIC!

Kent Vol I

Edited by Michelle Warrington

First published in Great Britain in 1999 by
POETRY NOW YOUNG WRITERS
1-2 Wainman Road, Woodston,
Peterborough, PE2 7BU
Telephone (01733) 230748

HB ISBN 0 75430 301 2
SB ISBN 0 75430 302 0

FOREWORD

With over 63,000 entries for this year's Cosmic competition, it has proved to be our most demanding editing year to date.

We were, however, helped immensely by the fantastic standard of entries we received, and, on behalf of the Young Writers team, thank you.

Cosmic Kent Vol I is a tremendous reflection on the writing abilities of 8 & 9 year old children, and the teachers who have encouraged them must take a great deal of credit.

We hope that you enjoy reading *Cosmic Kent Vol I* and that you are impressed with the variety of poems and style with which they are written, giving an insight into the minds of young children and what they think about the world today.

CONTENTS

THE POEMS

DRAGONS

Some dragons are tall, as tall as a mountain.
Some dragons are small, as small as a fly.
They can be fat, as fat as a pig,
They can be skinny, as skinny as straw.
They are dirty, like the dump,
And they are definitely nasty.
Dragons guard treasure,
Shiny gold treasure in a gloomy, dark cave.
Dragons like gold, shiny, gold blocks.
They also like snowflakes, filigree snowflakes,
When it is cold.
Dragons are stupid.
They are red, some are green.
Some can be blue, as blue as the sea.
Dragons have scales, a spine or two.
We really don't know. Do you?

Some dragons are fast, as fast as a car,
And some are slow, as slow as a snail.
A dragon has fiery breath, as hot as a cauldron.
We just don't know,
And they are gods of destruction.
Some are red, some are green
We just don't know. Do you?
Dragons are dangerous.
Some dragons are nice.
Their claws are hard and stiff,
Just like rock and ice.

David Whitecross (9)
Aycliffe CP School

Dragons

Dragons are fierce, mighty and brave,
They have smoke, fire and spikes,
Some are good and some are bad,
But I think they are bad.

He has wings for arms,
Claws for feet,
Spikes on top of his neck,
Big blue eyes,
Hot red fire,
And he is very scary.

But don't be scared,
Brave knight is here,
No more fire or smoke,
No, it will be heaven!

Kirsty Wickings (10)
Aycliffe CP School

Dragons

Dragons are sometimes fierce and horrible.
They swoop and land loudly, which makes people shiver.
Their big heavy tails and long scaly necks swoop over the blue skies,
With their glittering eyes as the dragons roam the land.

Their claws dig into the ground as they walk through the land.
In their caves they snore as they sleep.
Their teeth clatter as they sleep quietly.

Fire bursts out of their nostrils as they roar and growl,
But sometimes dragons are nice.

Selina Chiu (9)
Aycliffe CP School

THERE'S A DRAGON IN MY SCHOOL, MUM

'There's a dragon in my school, Mum,
He's huge and green.'

'Don't tell lies, dear
Go to bed please.'

'There's a dragon in my school, Mum,
and he's rough and tough.'

'Go to bed you little pest,
I don't want to hear anymore.'

'There's a dragon in my school, Mum,
he breathes hot fire.'

'Please shut up and go to bed,
I want to watch this programme.'

'There's a dragon in my school, Mum,
he roars like a bulldozer.'

'*Please,* please go to bed,
tell me in the morning.'

'Mum please.'

'Go to bed *now!*
Goodnight.'

Natasha Dawson (9)
Aycliffe CP School

MY PET MARTIAN

Once I went up into space,
And saw a Martian's funny face,
He had no nose,
But smelly toes,
He had three eyes,
Which looked like pies,
He had a beard,
Which looked a bit weird,
He had frizzy hair,
Quite like a bear.
Then the Martian made a jump
And landed with a great big thump,
He looked very hurt,
And covered in dirt,
I offered him one of my chocolate bars,
But instead he ate the whole of Mars,
Next he ate all of the moon,
And he was going to eat Pluto very soon,
Before he could a comet rushed past,
Knocking him, falling very fast,
He landed on a shiny star,
He had fallen really, really far,
I jumped in my rocket and I flew down,
I flew the Martian to my home town,
Then I took him to my house,
And I crept in as quiet as a mouse,
And I never did tell my mum and dad,
About the pet Martian I always had.

Matthew Potter (9)
Benenden Primary School

In Space

Floating through space
On a mysterious case.
So cold and black
Like the inside of a sack.
Nothing like cars,
But I'll visit stars and Mars.
Is it the end?
No, it's so never ending.
Nowhere to go.
I am feeling very low.
Strange and scary.
Aliens, very hairy.
Lots more rockets
Floating through space
Also on a giant case.
I'll try eating,
Oh no, it's not working.
There goes a chip,

Floating in space!

Philippa Doherty (9)
Benenden Primary School

Space

When I go and look out at night
The moon is so very bright.
A shooting star goes racing by
in the dark sky.
Oh I wonder how the star stays so high?

Katie Bowman (7)
Benenden Primary School

Planet Men

The man from Mars,
Collected some jam jars,
The man on Pluto,
Plays on his flute oh,
You should see the man on Jupiter,
Who plays on his computer,
The man on Mercury,
You should see how he hurt me,
The man on Saturn,
On his jumper he had a pattern,
The man from Uranus,
Had just bought some new trainers,
The man on the moon,
Was watching a cartoon,
The lady on Earth,
Had just given birth,
To a little baby boy,
Who gave a lot of joy.

Amy Fullwood (9)
Benenden Primary School

Stars

I saw a star up in the sky, and 25 men shooting by.
They looked suspicious, they looked sly.
I don't think I like them shooting by.

We wonder why these 25 men shot across the sky,
But maybe little green men from other planets have
A good reason why.

G Coxhead (8)
Benenden Primary School

Cosmic Crash

One day I was rocketing into outer space,
Looking for an alien, to have a great big chase.
Then in front of me I saw a big comet,
I wished I was at home watching Wallace and Gromitt.
I screwed up my eyes, and heard a big bang,
And that was followed, by a great clang.
The rocket smashed to pieces, as it hit the comet,
I felt I was a ball being used to play cricket.

I fell out of the door and met an alien,
By the sound of it he was Australian.
When I got to know him, he took me to a planet,
Where there was one thing from Earth, a gannet.
Then I saw a wormhole, quite a big one,
I wondered if I went through, I'd land on my mum.
I did! Oh I did! And she let out a shriek.
For more space adventures, see you next week.

Jonathan Hall (9)
Benenden Primary School

Moon, Moon

Moon, moon, oh how
I like to gaze at you.
Dazzling, so bright
Looking through my bedroom window
Morning dawns
I ask my mam
Where has the moon gone?

Jack O'Loughlin (8)
Benenden Primary School

Future Space

Travelling along the space highway
I've been travelling all night and now all day
Future space is a brilliant place
Alien cars rush by me
Aliens with more eyes than you want to see
Future space is a brilliant place
We call our time just future space
Where I am is as black as an ace
Future space is a brilliant place.

I pass some buildings at hyper-speed
In a race I'd be in the lead
Future space is a brilliant place
Now as I come up to Mars
I pass some brightly burning stars
Future space is a brilliant place.

Fred Francis (9)
Benenden Primary School

Planets

The moon is dark
The sun is bright
The planets are in the sky at night.

The cold of Pluto
The red of Mars
The storms of Venus
Make these planets our stars.

Rachel Boune (9)
Benenden Primary School

WAY UP THERE . . .

Way up there
aliens roam.
Way up there,
stars shine bright.
Way up there,
satellites scan.
Way up there,
comets zoom.
Way up there,
planets spin.
Way up there,
the future holds.

Oliver Burgess (9)
Benenden Primary School

ALIENS

UFOs hide in craters
Fighting intergalactic skaters
Lizard men live on Mars
Sitting in lovely spas
Star-troopers fighting nasty intergalactic
Party poopers
Darth Vader is the mean invader
Flying around in a cargo trader.

Elliot Ryan (8)
Benenden Primary School

Scary Martian

Astronauts go up and out and on the moon they float about.
Suddenly up in space they saw a tiny Martian face,
His body was green and he looked so mean.
Two antennae wriggled about and three eyes stared them out.
He had no nose but very large toes
And spots on his back that opened and closed.
The astronauts quickly went back to the rocket
As the Martians' eyes fell out of their sockets.
As the rocket took off there was a sigh of relief
They would all soon be home for a nice cup of tea.

Lauren Beeslee (7)
Benenden Primary School

Solar System

The solar system is big and black,
It's full of little aliens,
With little packs on little backs,
And planets so high in the sky.

The planets are Uranus and Saturn,
Jupiter, Mars, Pluto, Earth and Venus too,
And last of all there is Mercury and Neptune,
All stuck together with glue!

Harriet Brown (8)
Benenden Primary School

Space

Up, up in space there are aliens
With their ten eyes sticking out,
I don't suppose they have snouts.
When rockets come by, up in the sky
They all shout 'Look! Red people!'
When the rocket comes down
We can see what people look like,
They might have weird hair-do's
like cuckoo birds.

Amelia Edmonston (8)
Benenden Primary School

My Favourite Animals

I like animals
Fat and thin
Big and small
With a grin.

Leopards have spots
Wolves are grey or black and white
Lions are plain
And so are lynx.

My sister likes cats
And I like rabbits
But best of all
I love
My dog Rosie.

Jacob Barlow (7)
Chartfield School

ANIMALS

A nimals are lovely, I think it's true,
N ice to look at in the zoo,
I like horses, elephants and hares,
M onkeys, tigers and big bears.
A lligators are creepy and so are rats,
L ots get chased by fearsome cats.
S nakes are scary, just like bats.

Nikoo Sarrafan (8)
Chartfield School

SPRING

S is for a sunny day.
P is for a juicy pear.
R is for a ripe fruit.
I is for an ice-cream.
N is for a nice apple.
G is for a goat munching the juicy grass.

Alisdair Gilmour (9)
Chartfield School

THE WIND, THE RAIN AND THE SUN

The wind, the wind, swirls round and round
The rain, the rain, comes pouring down
The sun comes out and dries the rain
So that I can go out to play again.

Simon Anstice (8)
Chartfield School

My Hamster Joe

My hamster's called Joe,
He's very sweet, I know,
He goes very fast in his wheel,
He likes to eat apple peel,
My cat watches him from the window-sill,
At night and at day,
He washes his face.

My friends had him once,
While we went away.
They asked me if they could keep him,
But I said 'No.'
Because I love him
He's my hamster, *Joe!*

Anton Morigi (7)
Chartfield School

Spring Time

Spring is a time when baby lambs are born,
Skipping and jumping across the fields.
Days get longer and nights become shorter.
Daffodils start to grow and flowers begin to bloom.
The birds sing so merrily in the trees,
Below a carpet of bluebells we can see.
The blossom blows off the trees in the wind,
Showers in April come with the sun,
Making a rainbow so big and bright.
What a happy sight to see!

Sam Brill (8)
Chartfield School

My Pet Rabbits

I've got two pet rabbits
They live out in a hutch
They drink water from a bottle
And I love them very much.

One rabbit's called Flopsy
And he is black
He likes playing in the garden
And he hops like Jumping Jack.

The other's name is Thumper
He is black and white
He loves munching carrots
And they eat their food at night.

Oliver Towner (8)
Chartfield School

Harley

Harley is my puppy
He can be very mucky
He makes holes in clothes
And bites my toes
He likes to play
Especially in May
He scratches my socks
And chews his box
He jumps up
But he's only a pup
But I still love my puppy Harley.

Rachael Derbyshire (8)
Chartfield School

The Weather I Like Best

The weather is different
In all kinds of ways
Never is it the same
On any one day.

Sometimes it's sunny
And the wind blows,
Sometimes it rains
And in winter it snows.

I like it best
When it's sunny all day
And I can go out
In the garden to play.

Laura Crocker (8)
Chartfield School

The Mouldy Green Cheese

There's a green cheese in our fridge.
It's gone mouldy,
I used it in an experiment.
I put it in the back so nobody would
notice except me.
When my mum finds it,
I think I am going to be in trouble.

My mum lets out a scream,
I think that she must have found it.
Whatever will I do next?
However will I escape?
Green cheese is my doom!

Julian Campbell (9)
Chartfield School

MY RABBIT FLOPSY

Flopsy is grey and brown
It would be too dangerous to go into town
She is funny, she jumps so high
One day she will reach the sky.

She likes carrots to eat
When her nose twitches she looks so sweet
In the sunshine she loves to play
At night-time she snuggles in her hay.

Sometimes she is naughty and digs a hole
Daddy tells her off, poor soul!
So then I give her a treat.
She sits with me on the swinging seat.

Joseph Fusco (7)
Chartfield School

MY DOG ZELDA

My dog Zelda guards me at night,
My dog Zelda gives everyone a fright,
I love her,
Because she has soft fur.

I sometimes take Zelda for a walk,
And she absolutely loves pork,
I sure wish she could talk,
And tell me what it's like being a dog.

She loves to play and loves to run,
But most of all have fun,
She loves to lie in the sun,
And has been known to steal a bun.

Lawrence Rose (8)
Chartfield School

Matches, Matches

Matches, Matches
never touch, they can burn you very much.

Matches, Matches
light your fire, while you sit by your warm cosy fire.

Matches, Matches
are not fun because they can burn you,
now that's not fun!

Kyra Gifford (9)
Dame Janet CP School

I Like Lying On My Bed

I like lying on my bed,
Thinking of what I said.
I like playing my Game Boy.
I am good and certainly not coy.
My scores are great.
Better than my mate.

Scott Corke (8)
Dame Janet CP School

Chocolate

Chocolate is a nice big slice
All moist and brown
A quick drink to help it go down.

Dean Gleadale-Siddall (9)
Dame Janet CP School

Tick-Tock

Tick-tock.
Tick-tock.
My brother's clock.
Tick-tock.
Tick-tock.
There goes the clock.
Tick-tock.
Tick-tock.
Time to get up.
Time to get going.
Tick-tock.
Tick-tock.
Time to go.
Time to go.
Tick-tock.
Tick-tock.

Emma Hewitt (8)
Dame Janet CP School

Arnold

Arnold, Arnold, he's our man
He drives down the street in a proper man's van,
With a black and white cat sitting on his hat.
Riding down the hill singing 'Hey Diddly Do.'

Maxwell Mursell (9)
Dame Janet CP School

THE SPACE ROBOTS

Ten happy space robots flying in space
One ran out of fuel then there were nine.

Nine happy space robots looking at books
One blew up then there were eight.

Eight happy space robots eating space sweets
One went for more then there were seven.

Seven happy space robots playing on a space shuttle,
One fell overboard, then there were six.

Six happy space robots in a space maze,
One got lost then there were five.

Five happy space robots went home,
Then there were none.

Christopher Findeis (9)
Dame Janet CP School

THE MORNING FLOWER

The morning flower once in June will show its pretty
Petals under the moon.
The morning flower was not found
People looked all over the ground.
Then one day
In the month of May
The morning flower was found
But not on the ground.
It was up in a tree
Guarded by me.

Laura Jane Drake (9)
Dame Janet CP School

I Live In Space

I live in space.
It is a lovely place to be.
You can see Mars, Earth, Mercury, Pluto
And the other ones.
But now I think it's time for a change
So I am going to take a trip around the planets.
First of all you see *Mars*
Before you know it
You're on *Earth*
Then you are at *Mercury*.
Then you're at *Pluto*.
After that you're at *Saturn*.
You see that *Saturn* is smiling at you.
Crash!
Bump!
You've landed on the *Sun*.
Oh no!
If you don't get off the *Sun* you
will be fried!
Oh no!
The rocket won't move!
Help!
Help!
You have to get out of the rocket
To push it off the *Sun*.
I rush in the rocket
Finally you get home.
You say to yourself
I never want to go on a trip around
the planets again!

Mary Poynter (7)
Davington CP School

Aliens' Luggage

The galaxy, Milky Way and Mars,
Jupiter, Pluto as well.
Shiny stars and sparkling moon.
You can see the sun and moon.
Planets, comets, rockets and singing aliens
Astronaut flying too.

The Milky Way is here to stay
Don't you make him jump
Or he will have a massive bump.
Now you see the alien is very scary
So don't you mess with an alien
Or you know what will happen!

Sophie Harrison (7)
Davington CP School

Mars

I was looking up at the stars.
Suddenly I found myself on Planet Mars!
I must have wished I was here
Hey! But this doesn't seem like a sphere!
Planet Mars is square, I declare.

Elizabeth Bishop (7)
Davington CP School

Untitled

I'm in a rocket, I see the moon, and I
Zoom.
I see the stars
And the planet Mars.
I can see an alien ship.
I'm scared,
But nobody cared.
I don't think the sun
Was much fun.
So I went home
To my room.

India Guthrie (6)
Davington CP School

Cosmic

Look! Look outside! There is a light!
We went outside. It took me up into Jupiter.
I was scared! More aliens! Aliens! Aliens!
You haven't ever seen an alien scarier than this!
He greeted 'Hello' and then 'Goodbye'
I went home and went to bed.

Philippa Lethbridge (6)
Davington CP School

My Space Poem

I want to go to a place.
It would probably be space.
I would like to get there at a fast pace.
It was about to go from the ground.
My mum and dad were dancing all around.
I went past the sun, the moon,
A lot of stars, Jupiter and Mars.

Megan Harlow (7)
Davington CP School

Noises

One cold night in the spooky moonlight
All the stars are shining bright.

Howling foxes very frightening
Big loud crashes of thunder and lightning.

Rain is falling on the roof tops
People standing in doorways of shops.

Hear the engines of the cars
Vans and lorries driving past.

Where they are going, I don't know
There are lots of places they can go.

When I stand and listen
I hear noises near and far.

So stop, look, listen around you
Do you know what the noises are?

Christopher Bean (8)
Eastchurch Primary School

Space

Space is a wonderful sight,
With all the planets in it.

Jupiter the biggest one of all,
And Saturn isn't very small.

Mercury the hottest,
Pluto is the coldest.

Mars has seen,
That Uranus is green.

Venus at second place,
Neptune says it's not a race.

Earth is home to the human race,
Is there anybody else in space?

Katherine Ritchie (9)
East Stour CP School

Universe

Mercury so close to the sun,
Venus the hottest planet,
Earth our home,
Mars so brightly coloured,
Jupiter the biggest planet,
Saturn with its layers of dust rings,
Uranus such a turquoise colour,
Neptune so blue like the sea,
Pluto, the coldest planet,
Our universe is beautiful with its
galaxies.

Emma Turner (8)
East Stour CP School

FORSYTHIA

A bell dancing in on the golden tree.
A honey skirt swaying in the primrose air.
Shiny tassles droop.
A lemon door opening smoothly.
Crinkled leaves twist on primrose floor.
Coffee walnut twinkles the fine work.
The branch loops over the spine.

Susan Fedder (8)
Great Chart CP School

WINTER

The owl flutters in the wind
While snowballs echo past
Snowmen sob
Icicles melt in the cold
The snowmen shiver in the cold wind
Snow ploughs drag the snow away.

Alexander Dalton (8)
Great Chart CP School

LIGHTNING

Silver lightning sprints like a comet.
White hair snow flies over the moon
Speedy rockety zigzags flash in the night,
While the thunder growls with a lion's roar
Buttery electric heat strikes at a rapid pace.

Jack Bundock (9)
Great Chart CP School

Over The Top

My raw ear splinters,
A deafening shell.
Hunching back and flinching,
Inside the cruel hell.

From the trenches,
Showers the flare.
Like a violet firework,
With a violent blare.

Inside the dugout,
The soldier sat.
His bleeding nails,
Gnawed by rat.

Skeletal trees,
Sing their mournful song,
Of the firing bullets,
All the day long.

The General called,
I heard him say;
'Over the top,'
We must make our way.

The General called,
The General said,
But all men obey,
Are as good as the dead.

But over the top we walked,
Our rifles now our stings,
We are but slaves for slaughter,
Our General now our king.

On we ran,
Through artillery fire,
On we trudged,
Through corroded barbed wire.
I staggered like a drunk warthog,
My limbs they felt like lead,
Crimson stained my greatcoat.
I buckled, then fell down dead.

We looked around our graveyard,
All the ground was mud.
We stared at other bodies,
Their sides were caked in blood.

All I see is dying,
All I feel is pain.
All I hear is death,
Deserted in the rain.

Patrick Williams
Great Chart CP School

My Mum's Dream

You dream of travelling to the Caribbean Islands
and day-dreaming in a hammock on
the golden sand.
You dream of watching the turquoise sea
that lies like a blanket covering the
rough coral reef,
By pine brown palm trees.
You dream of jumping into the navy sea
and swimming around the tropical fish.

Ingrid Alder (8)
Great Chart CP School

Exotic Dream

My mum dreams of exotic blue seas
Along the Caribbean coast.
The volcanic sun burns into pale smooth skin
Lime green palm trees dangle over golden sands
Silver waves splash into glacier pools
Gold and orange citrus fruits sparkle in the breeze
Dolphins dive in cool glittering seas
Crabs scuttle around for shade
Mermaids make my mum Queen, Queen of the
Caribbean island.

Ahh! Paradise!

Kelly Gordon (9)
Great Chart CP School

Forsythia

Petals curl into arches of gold.
Shining velvet buttercups spread.
Their buds prance as gritty wood grows.
Delicate bells dance in the wind
Like gleaming lemons.
They bounce and twist in the
Crescent moon.

Laura Helen Cook (8)
Great Chart CP School

Holly Poem

The smooth pill rolls in green leaf
Loop marble bends
Sharp hill pricks like a pin
The smooth round pea shines
Green hedgehog cuts through the flame.
Football slopes pointing the green cream leaf.
Sharp pencil waves in the poppy marble.
The sun is blazing round the smooth prickly leaf.
Plump smooth starlight moon pointed at the prickly cave.

Jessica McLaughlin (8)
Great Chart CP School

Mother's Dream

A diver dives in the aquamarine sea,
She swims as a dolphin.
The dolphin makes bubbles as it flips up
Dolphins go zooming in the transparent water
It is flipping around in circles.
My mummy feels really happy and overjoyed
And really pleased seeing dolphins and whales.

Sam Reynolds (9)
Great Chart CP School

PERSEPHONE

She leaves a way of blossom
Petals fall on the silky grass
The breeze rustles the meadows
Footpaths of flowers sing 'Persephone'
Lambs play while Persephone dances
Birds fly over Persephone
Grass rustles while whispering 'Persephone'
Echoes come back of her mum's cry.

Benjamin Young (9)
Great Chart CP School

WINTER

The twinkling icicles are cold as snowfalls.
The whistling snow glitters in the soundless wind.
The moon glows in the twilight and the
Owl flutters his wings.
The dancing secret frost sobs.
The clocks of snow are silent.
Dark blizzard is chilly as it goes away.
Christmas is here as happiness comes.

Katie Arends (9)
Great Chart CP School

MY BABY BROTHER

My baby brother is so small,
He hasn't even learned to crawl.
He's only been around a week,
And all he seems to do is bawl
And wiggle, sleep . . . and leak!

Michaela Kirwan (9)
Hampton Primary School

PLANET WRITING

I know an alien, she is called Star,
And she has four arms and three legs on each side.
So if you get too close - she might eat you all up.
Her eyes are red and black like glowing coal.

She can be mean sometimes, but most of the time she is kind.
She's got webbed feet and hands.
Her hair is purple, red, blue, and black and plenty more.
She's a clever alien - crusty as well!
She gobbled up a girl called Sue and her Mum cried for five years.
By then my friend had gone back to Planet Writing
Where she lived . . .

The Planet Writing is very weird,
All they do is write and play.
It's a very dark blue
You can't see it at night
'Cos it's the same colour
As the sky.
It's got a big sign saying
Planet Writing!

Natasha Barleycorn (9)
Hampton Primary School

THE PUPPIES OF PLUTO

The puppies of Pluto play all day and night.
The puppies of Pluto are like bears in a fight!
They wrestle like mad
And they smash up their hot dog van
Steal the fried dog and the man.

Jamie Robertson (8)
Hampton Primary School

The Frogle From Mars!

A Frogle in a saucer
Landed in my front yard.
I think it was a Frogle - I'm sure it was a Frogle.
It looked like a Frogle with a shawl and pants on.
The pants were red and the shawl was blue.
It was eating a fish not fried or grilled just now.
The Frogle was green with orange eyes.
He is ten feel tall.
His nose is like jelly.
And his mouth is smelly,
His skin is rough and red.
He has purple fingers on each hand.
And moves in beautiful graceful leaps.
'Gubble, bub, shum, do danah!' he says.
I named him Hoper - he jumped for joy about his name.
He saw my friend and said 'How gah do you gala!'
On his last visit he bought a hat that was
Blue and then danced under the light of the moon.

Clare Stockley (9)
Hampton Primary School

Out Of This World

I'm in a rocket going to space.
I wonder if there's a place to land.
Because there's the Moon, Saturn,
Venus, Mars and more.
It sounds delicious with these names
Mars, Galaxy and the Milky Way!

Ryan Farrant (9)
Hampton Primary School

Out Of This World

In our spaceship off we go
Past the moon we are going slow.
Landing with a terrifying bump!
Green and blue aliens we find
Then I stand in some gungy slime.
We saw some glittering shining stars.
Then we see beautiful Mars.
Another astronaut sitting trying to communicate with an alien.
Time to go back to earth.
Bye to aliens - off we go!
Leaving space - we are going low
Drifting, drifting - now we're going too slow!

Natalie Stockley (9)
Hampton Primary School

Up In Space

Jupiter, Venus and Mars
The sun, the moon and the stars.
The sky is blue
The clouds are white
And the moon is made of cheese
The stars are made of buttons
And that's what I believe!

Charlotte Ellis (7)
Hampton Primary School

Out Of This World

As I look into the sky at night
And wonder about that beautiful light.
It could be the sun
It could be the moon - or
It could be a star shining down on you.
I often wonder if there's anyone
Looking down at me from the sun.
There could be a creature on the moon.
Waving down to me or you!

Kerry Rowland (7)
Hampton Primary School

One Morning

There he was
This little man
He was green
With a yellow hand
He said 'Hello!
But we've got to go.
I'm in a race
To outer space.'

Tanya Parsons (7)
Hampton Primary School

Out Of This World

I saw something in the garden
Shaped a bit like cars!
My mum and dad said they were spaceships
And could have been from Mars.
They were white with wings
But didn't have stings
And the creatures that drove them
Had legs and arms
And just had fingers - no palms.

Lucy Capon (8)
Hampton Primary School

Aliens And Monsters

Up in space the aliens and monsters
gather around everytime.
Someone comes from earth.
To see if they are three eyed or two eyed
To see how many legs they have!
To see how many heads they have!
In space at morning - the aliens and monsters
all go to sleep and wake up at night.

Richard Miller (8)
Hampton Primary School

Out Of This World

Up in space it is dirty and cold
I look at the stars with a smiling face
I look at the earth far far below
People come to visit me each year
People zoom in rockets around me
Blowing me round and round
They tell me what happens below
They talk to me for a minute
Then back to earth they go!

Natalie Sheppard (8)
Hampton Primary School

My Adventure In Space

I saw a light in the sky.
It was so big and bright.
But when it landed on my house
It did give me a fright.
A little man with six fingers and toes
Flew down by my side.
He invited me for tea
And we had green pancakes.

Kim Vass (7)
Hampton Primary School

Gorilla

Sits about a lot
Moves around very slowly
Big, fat and hairy.

Charlotte Andrew (8)
Harcourt Primary School

My Brother

I like my brother.
Funny, annoying, fair, round
Plays with cars and coins.

John Godden (8)
Harcourt Primary School

Sweets

I love sweets too much.
Fruity, brilliant, solid.
They are big and small.

Andrew Kennish (8)
Harcourt Primary School

My Friend

I like Claire Reilly
She likes to play with me lots
Trustful, helpful - fun.

Danielle Bevan (8)
Harcourt Primary School

Uncle Dave And D's

Uncle Dave woke up one morning
With a very strange disease.
He found he could only do things that began with the letter 'd'.
Uncle Dave said to Danny 'Ding, Dan, dog!'
He said 'What a loud of nonsense'
And sent him to the doctor.
Doctor said 'I think you've gone down with a *'d'* disease'
When Uncle got home he said
'Delightful dog, disgusting donkey, diving duck,'
'Dinner' said David driving down the drive.
'Delicious dinner' said Uncle Dave.
Next day Uncle Dave drove to the doctors.
Doctor said 'We have a cure!'
And he did!

Sarah Bliss (9)
Harcourt Primary School

Untitled

I like Miss Tredwell
Because she gives me hard work.
Reading, writing and sums!

Dennis Richardson (8)
Harcourt Primary School

Swimming

I love my swimming
Because I can go under
Wiggly, water shapes.

Adam Tuck (8)
Harcourt Primary School

Trees

Trees are lovely
The shades of leaves,
Green, red, brown, yellow.
Swaying in the breeze
The birds use them to build their nests.
High up in the branches.
To protect them from pests.
Squirrels love them.
Jumping from branch to branch,
It's very hard to see them.
They're very fast.
So please look after our trees.
They're very special things.
They're home for many animals.
Especially ones with wings.

Jenna Hart (9)
Harcourt Primary School

The Baby Dragon

He's a baby - just a baby.
Yes! A little, little baby.
He bites, he nibbles
But he never ever dribbles.
He's kind, he cares and he
Never ever stares.
He always bumps his head
On his little, little bed.
He's got wings on his side
And he hasn't got much pride.

Cara Copeland (8)
Perry Hall Primary School

OH! CHRISTMAS DAY IS COMING

Oh! hurrah! it's Christmas morning!
Fa, la, la . . .
Get up and quit that yawning!
Fa, la, la . . .
Christmas pudding, with custard!
Fa, la, la . . .
Turkey with sauce, and mustard!
Fa, la, la . . .
Cream potatoes, with gravy!
Fa, la, la . . .
Cold food, and savoury!
Fa, la, la . . .
Brussel sprouts, with cheese!
Fa, la, la . . .
Ice-cream, to make you freeze!
Fa, la, la . . .
Hot bread, with butter!
Fa, la, la . . .
Not a thing to make you splutter!
Fa, la, la . . .
Chocolate bars, and sweets!
Fa, la, la . . .
A hamper full of treats!
Fa, la, la . . .
All the wine you could desire!
Fa, la, la . . .
As you drink it by the fire!
Fa, la, la . . .
Cranberry sauce and rum!
Fa, la, la . . .
Oh! isn't dinner fun!
For one and all . . .

Alexandra Poulter (9)
Perry Hall Primary School

SCHOOL

Oh! my gosh it is nine o'clock.
Got to get to school,
Got to hurry up!
In come the teachers
For another day's work!
They are looking a little tired,
I wonder if they have marked my
Homework!
I have a feeling in my head
They are going to say
'Your homework is dreadful - it is scruffy and pathetic.
But then again it is just a thought
I'm sure everything will be all right!
'Frostie! come up here'
Oh no! I think
'Don't worry it is just your holiday form
Not a clip round the ear!'
The bell has rang - *I* say *yippee!*
Now we can go home and have some tea!

Ben Frost (8)
Perry Hall Primary School

MY BEST FRIEND

My best friend is easy to please
My best friend is easy to tease
My best friend has dark green eyes
My best friend doesn't tell lies
My best friend stays with me
My best friend looks like me!

Chloe Jones (9)
Perry Hall Primary School

A Day At The Beach

I love to run along the sand
And play with my red ball.
To splash with my friends - hand in hand
In the water to keep cool.

We wandered down to see the pier
And to take in the sea air.
My dad decides to have a beer
While we wander round the fair.

We settled on a nice ice-cream
Before the donkey ride,
I was picked for the rounders' team
When we won - I was full of pride.

As I looked up the sky was black
And as the rain came down.
We hurriedly put on our new Macs
And made for the chip shop in the town!

Alissa Mears (9)
Perry Hall Primary School

The Alien Took My Clothes

Early one morning on Monday
Mum pegged out clothes she had washed on Sunday.
Then a spaceship came down with a crash.
And an alien appeared - in a flash!
He took my dress off the line - back to space.
You should have seen the look on mum's face.

Claire Spearman (8)
Perry Hall Primary School

Penguins

Penguins walk in the crispy snow.
Waiting for people to pass by.
A penguin waits while another slides.
A person at last runs by.
The children throw snowballs in a fight.
But the ice cracks and the children go.
The penguins also begin to slow.
The children run home in fright.
But the penguins started off in flight.
The children eat.
One climbed to her feet.
She began to scream.
Our hair nearly flew off.
While our hands flew off
And to our amazement
We were flying too!

Sophie Sam (8)
Perry Hall Primary School

Lights

Candle lights, car lights
Torch lights and distance lights
Lighthouse lights near lights
Shaped lights and children's party lights.

Coloured lights, street lights, tall lights
Small lights, star lights
Pop lights, game lights and show lights
And cinema lights.
All lights can help us!

Emma Shiel (8)
Perry Hall Primary School

The Proud Peacock

I am the *proud peacock!*

I don't only have one hundred plumes,
I have two thousand plumes with eyes like stars!

I don't eat seeds and grass,
I eat the guards and the cherry-buns
They have in the restaurant - *Ambers!*

I don't sleep in the garden shed,
I sleep in the Queen of Spain's spare bed!

I don't dress myself in bugs and weeds,
I dress in the Queen's satin and fur evening beads.

Because I am the *proud peacock!*

Hayley Elsley (9)
Perry Hall Primary School

The Strangest Mouse I've Ever Seen!

I'm the mouse - the strangest mouse.
I don't eat: Wheat!
I eat: Crocodiles specially their feet!
I don't drink: Water
I drink: Dracular blood only if it's sweet.
I don't chase: Elephants!
I chase: Brian Moses just for his stories and poems.
I don't live: In a hole!
I live: Up the king's pyjamas even when he's asleep.
I told you I was strange - are you as strange as me?

Joanna Cachia (9)
Perry Hall Primary School

ALIEN

When an alien came down to earth
It took my plants that were in some turf
When I went to stand on the ground
He took something that he had found
I hid everything that he was going to get
I still haven't had my dinner yet
When he went back to space
I fell over and cut my face
I said that I will miss him
But he was too busy singing a hymn.

Samantha Brand (8)
Perry Hall Primary School

A ROOFTOP

A rooftop dreams of flying.
Of jumping off the building and
Gliding through the air.
It dreams of looping the loop,
Of flying to the south in winter,
It dreams of migrating its tiles
And flying higher and higher into the air.
Of cutting lamp posts in half when it flies by.
It dreams of meeting another rooftop
And laying eggs and having a family.

Christopher Lawrence (9)
Perry Hall Primary School

The Rapid Rhino

I'm the *rapid rhino!*
I don't eat grass.
I eat fish and lion cubs,
I don't drink water,
I drink slime!
I don't sleep on grass,
I sleep on Mars!
I don't chase humans,
I chase space aliens!
That's me! The rapid rhino.

Daniel Lockyer (9)
Perry Hall Primary School

Breeze

Gentle, calm weather,
Look at the sun!

Playing on the beach,
Isn't it fun?

Sand brushes on my face,
'Come on let's go.'

'Do up your lace.'
Sun sinks low into space.

Red, yellow, purple.
The breeze blows through my hair,

As up into the clouds,
I stand and stare.

Flavia Baker-Farr (9)
Petham County Primary School

Hurricane Storming

Smashing, bashing winds are crashing,
Together making rumbles.
Wildly piling, not at all smiling
Downstairs furniture tumbles.

Lightning flaming furiously
Wind is blowing it out.
Wind's victorious, but not for long
Lightning gives him a clout.

Slashing, spitting, hissing rain
Is starting to bucket from high
Thunder's wicked, lightning's cracking
Electricity from up in the sky.

Wind is howling and pushing hard
And wind is whistling, whirling
Thunder gives a great big bang
Then something gets to twirling.

Trees are cracking and smashing
And leaves are scattered about
Look at all the whistling, whirling wind
As kicks from bad weather start to spout.

The wind drops and the rain stops
And it's the end of the storm!

All of us 'Yay!'
We shout 'Oh! hurray'
Because it is *finished!*

Sarah Ventress (8)
Petham County Primary School

STORM

Thunder punches
Trips and leaps
Flashing and fighting
Jumping and rushing
Rumbling and crushing
Blowing
Lighting.

Luke Ilott (9)
Petham County Primary School

WIND

Wind howls,
Claws in the night.
Wind is cold,
Alive in the night.
Icy rain,
Wet rain,
Pours in the night!

Laurissa Adams (9)
Petham County Primary School

TORNADO

Scraping everything in its path.
Killing everything in its way
Swooping things into the sky
Ripping walls into the air
Tossing everything into the heavens!

Sean Bishop (9)
Petham County Primary School

Storm

Dragons roar
Lightning crashes
Trees fall
Wind bashes

Walls break
Windows shatter
Mad storm
Winds batter

Lightning whips
Rain pours
Thunder deafens
Biting claws

Lightning stops
Rain decreases
Wind drops
Thunder ceases.

Tobias Showan (9)
Petham County Primary School

The Wind And Rain

The wind punches your face,
Like Jack Frost's fist.

The ground is as wet as a bog,
Frosty patterns like hands spread on the ground.

Rain lashes like a wild sea,
And the wind is as strong as a giant's breath.

Emma Cardno (9)
Petham County Primary School

Tornado

I crash through the villages, towns and cities.
I swirl around anything that dares to be in that area.
I'm the king of the weather, no matter what
Because I tower above them as high as can be,
And I get wider the higher I go.
I'm lacking much more than I deserve,
Because people and things rise up me like an elephant herd!
My strength is so high, I lift up a house
And terrify the living creatures.
I'm crashing through houses, I never dig down.
I just lift
and
suck
and
swirl!

Ben Kinnersley (8)
Petham County Primary School

My Family

My mother is like the peel of a potato.
My brother is like a blasting volcano.
My mother gives me lots of wishes.
My father pays for the satellite dishes.
My mother makes me act like a chef.
My brother annoys me nearly to death.
My mother is as gentle as a hippopotamus.
My father is as angry as a rhinoceros!

Sophie Robertson (8)
Petham County Primary School

Tornado

Night-time
Crash!
The roof ripped off!

I run downstairs.
The roof has *gone!*

A funnelling Tornado!
Colliding into the sitting room.
A mass of bricks.

I run outside.
A rumble.
It was gone.

There was so much damage!

Alexander Brazier (7)
Petham County Primary School

A Christmas Night

Christmas puddings covered in cream.
Henry opens his presents under the tree.
Riddles behind the door,
In the sitting room a shiny tree.
Santa's here with his sleigh.
'Time for bed' says mum.
'Must we?' they say.
'Yes you must, Santa's on his way.'

Rosie Hosker (7)
Petham County Primary School

WINTER

Snow - white bright
and dazzling
frozen water
into ice
cold and frozen
lips sore
nose red
fingers numb
children making snowballs
and snowmen
children crying out and shouting
crunching snow under your feet
happy people in the snow.

Maria Jakeman (8)
Petham County Primary School

HURRICANE

Trees *crashing* on the ground.
Slates *flying* off houses.
Lightning *crashes*
Thunder *roars*
Blood thumping
Windows *smash*
Power cuts
Across the town!

Joshua Pugh (7)
Petham County Primary School

HURRICANE

Hurricane
Devastating
Devastating things.
Crashing the rooftops.
Bashing in the sides.
Terrifying the people inside.
Breaking tall houses.

The hurricane is feared
And
always
will be!

Jacob Moore (8)
Petham County Primary School

MY LITTLE SISTER

My little sister is a funny kind of thing
One moment she's crying the next she's laughing
My little sister is a funny kind of thing
One moment she's singing the next she's sleeping.

My little sister is a funny kind of thing
One moment she's dancing the next she's singing
My little sister is a lovely kind of thing
My little sister is everything.

Katrina Caplan (8)
Petham County Primary School

All Day Raining

Grey inside
Grey outside
No games to play
Raindrops are see-through
Boring inside, fun outside
It's raining all day!

Grey clouds overhead
Looks like it's going to pour
Splash
The first button raindrops fall
Out of the cloud of grey.

Emma Jo Bulpitt (8)
Petham County Primary School

Rain

Slushing and gushing
Down the drain
Puddles glistening
In the rain.
Rain is plain
Just grey and damp.
Rain feels squelchy
Cold and wet.
It feels soggy in your shoes.
Rain pounds at the windows
Rushing towards you.

Emily Martindale (9)
Petham County Primary School

Spring Holiday

May's the month of sun and showers
Skies of blue and clouds of grey
Springing grass and nodding flowers
Streams that whisper, come away!

May's the month when days grow longer
Fled old winter's sudden chill
Come away! The call seems stronger
From the distant, dreaming hill.

May's the months when blossom falling
Soon we'll take our holidays
Heather clad, the moors are calling
Birds are singing 'Come away!'

Sophie Paynter (9)
Poverest Primary School

Waiting

I'm waiting for spring when the buttercups come up and I know there's one more season until summer. Spring is the refreshing season for flowers to grow and snow to melt. I can't wait until spring so it's warm instead of cold. I'm waiting for the weekend so I can watch Friday Night Comedy Zone and there's nothing I like better than Arnold Schwarzenegger after a hard day's work. So I'm waiting I'm waiting I'm waiting.

Jak Jones (9)
Poverest Primary School

A HAPPY POEM

My dad makes me happy
because he buys me things
like
sweets and chocs
in a great big box.
My dad makes me happy
because he lets me stay up late
and watch things on the telly
I think he's great.
My dad makes me happy
because he wears bright trousers
and they make other people smile.
I like to walk beside him
because they make me laugh.
My dad makes me happy
because he cooks nicely
and the food tastes nice.
It makes my tummy warm.
My dad makes me happy
because he is good.
He helps me with bullies.
He helps me with my homework
Which is usually right.
My dad makes me happy
because he loves me
lots
and I
love him too.

Damien Bateman (9)
Poverest Primary School

Floating About In Space

S pace is cold and dark
P acing about in space
A s it's such fun
C osmical, so it is
E specially when you go and see the moon.

Sam Baker (8)
St Francis RC Primary School, Maidstone

Mission Control

Mission control, it's very dark up here.
I'm in a moon buggy right now.
I'm very hot up here.
Mission control, I will see you in twenty years,
But for now, over and out.

Nathan Pollard-Fraser (8)
St Francis RC Primary School, Maidstone

Cosmic

Planets, planets do you smile
Like the man in the moon?
Do you have water?
Do you have air?
Could I live there?

Andrew Cott (9)
St Francis RC Primary School, Maidstone

Looking Around In Space

Looking around at a scary dark place,
Seeing all the planets that are there,
Looking around in the emptiness out here in space,
Seeing rockets and the moon floating in space,
It is so empty out there in space.

Sophie Vinall (8)
St Francis RC Primary School, Maidstone

Floating Away In Space

Jumping out of my shuttle or a rocket as you might call it.
Floating past a lot of planets, some with aliens on.
I might teach them football or they might teach me their language.
Space station, is there any room on the moon for me?
Callum O'Brien over and out.

Callum O'Brien (8)
St Francis RC Primary School, Maidstone

People In Space

People in space look very strange. I call them aliens.
In my spaceship it was very different from my home.
The food tastes different, I don't like it.
It tastes disgusting.
Then I went and said hello to the aliens and we played.

Charlotte Denton (7)
St Francis RC Primary School, Maidstone

JUNGLES

In the jungle you will see
A small baby monkey just like me
Swinging in the trees.

In the jungle you will see
A lion roaring
Just like me.

In the jungle you will see
A little giraffe as tall as you
It's like a giant.

In the jungle you will see
A baby elephant with its mum
Cuddling each other
Walking like elephants.

In the jungle you will see
Some hunters trying to kill the animals
Big or small.

Kathleen Durling (8)
St Francis RC Primary School, Maidstone

OUT IN SPACE

Out in the darkness of space
Passing all the planets
No humans in space?

Out in the darkness of space
All cold and creepy
The world below looks like a football
spinning round.

Dale Owen (7)
St Francis RC Primary School, Maidstone

Cosmic

I'm flying in my spaceship
From the world I want to go
A planet I want to stand on
Then aliens I really will know.
There's something at the window
I see an ugly face
I think it is a monster
From outer space.
I'm pushing these buttons
I'm going higher and
I see some wire
Sticking out of my engine.
I'm twirling up and up
I'm really going high and
I'm seeing the stars.
I landed on Mars
Then I twirl and twirl down to the ground
Because my engine has made no sound.

Katie Highwood (8)
St Francis RC Primary School, Maidstone

Space

Is there room on the moon for me?
Is it cold and empty?
I'm up and floaty in the air.
Yes, it's dark and scary up there.
It's open like a door
And rockets spin around like mad.
When I went to Mars I saw an alien's grave place.
I fainted on the floor when the alien rose.

Rebecca Fanning (7)
St Francis RC Primary School, Maidstone

Cosmic

When I was in space
I saw a monster
When I was in space
I saw an alien
When I was in space
I saw planet Earth
When I was in space
I saw planet Mars
When I was in space
I saw the sun
When I was in space
I saw the moon
When I was in space
I saw Pluto
When I was in space
I saw a spaceship.

Andre Lebrette (8)
St Francis RC Primary School, Maidstone

Floating Around In Space

Floating around in space
Feeling apart from my friends
And the whole human race.
It's dark up here.
'Hello mission control, help me out.
I'm now in space.
See you in twenty years,
Over and out.'

Emily Neller (8)
St Francis RC Primary School, Maidstone

Mission Control

Mission control do you read me?
I really don't take too much room.
Mission control do you need me
On the next rocket to space?

I really want to go to Mars
One day I was so pleased
Because I was going to Mars
When I got in the rocket
My mum said to me
'I really want to go to Mars.'

So mission control do you read me?
I really don't take too much room
Mission control do you need me
On the next rocket to Mars?

Charlotte Green (7)
St Francis RC Primary School, Maidstone

Cosmic

Space, space can you see
I like space
It likes me
More and more
A planet turns around
I hear a big sound
Round and round
I cannot stop spinning
Around and around.

Danielle Clucas (9)
St Francis RC Primary School, Maidstone

Cosmic

One day I was sitting under a tree
In a dark forest.
A spaceship landed beside me.
A purple man with green eyes
Took me up to heaven.
It was a very happy place.
It was all white.
Then we had a ride in the spaceship
Around space.
We came down down.
He told me his name. It was Fred!
I said thank you to Fred.
My mum called me
Into my house.
I was home!

Paul Savage (8)
St Francis RC Primary School, Maidstone

Space

I looked through a telescope.
I saw space, it was dark like a cat.
Astronauts were floating along.
The astronauts asked 'Where do you come from?'
I said I came from earth.
I said I needed to go.
I will visit you again.

Tessa Kadicheeni (8)
St Francis RC Primary School, Maidstone

Farms

I know a farm
That rests on the moor
With ninety-nine horses
We could add one more

I know a farm
That rests in the sky
It really surprises me
How a farm can fly

I know a farm
That's a million miles away
It will come to earth
In a year and a day.

Caroline Gregory (8)
St Francis RC Primary School, Maidstone

Babies!

Babies scream, babies wail,
Sometimes they pull the cat's tail.
Babies cry, babies scribble,
And they dribble on their bibble.
Babies wee, babies poo,
Who's going to change the nappy?
You!

Thomas Black (8)
St Francis RC Primary School, Maidstone

The Singing Family

I am a dog, I live in a dirty house.
It's so dirty, I get the blame for having dirty paws.
My owners are very funny because they sing in the bath.
No wonder we're called 'the singing family'.
I am a spotty dog, so when I get dirty
they think they've got another dog.

Fiona Cassidy (7)
St Francis RC Primary School, Maidstone

A Hamster

A hamster is small like a rolled up ball
It's soft, so sweet, and eats and peeps
So sweet it leaps.
It has small little eyes, long fur
And small little feet,
They are so pink they make me wink.

Carly Maidment (9)
St John's CE Primary School, Sevenoaks

Rabbits Are

Rabbits, rabbits are soft and furry
They're sweet and cool
They eat hay every day

Rabbits, rabbits hop like frogs
Sit like dogs.

Samantha Marchant (8)
St John's CE Primary School, Sevenoaks

Cats

Cats purr
Cats miaow
Cats are fluffy and puffy
Cats creep round the streets
Cats lick and pick
Cats are rough
Cats are soft
Cats are cute, just like you
Cats scratch
Cats snatch.

Rebecca Phillips (9)
St John's CE Primary School, Sevenoaks

A Cat

A cat chases mice
In gardens and indoors.
My cat loves mice.
He spies on you.
You will never know
What he gets up to
When you go out.

Andrea Seal (8)
St John's CE Primary School, Sevenoaks

CATS

Cats miaow, they miaow out loud.
Cats purr and they have a lot of fur.
Cats are fluffy and very puffy.
Cats have paws and on their paws
They have very sharp claws.
Cats sit on anyone's lap and
Cats can drink out of a tap.
Cats eat mice and maybe
Cats might cat some woodlice.

Cally Sims (8)
St John's CE Primary School, Sevenoaks

HELP!

Help there's a crocodile,
Help there's a fierce tree,
Help there's a monkey,
And they're going to eat me.

Help the tree's got me,
There's a bee,
It lives in a tree,
I want to go home.

Liza Bashford (9)
St John's CE Primary School, Sevenoaks

I REMEMBER

I remember the new blue sky as high as I am now
and the sun as bright as its own light.
The breeze is flowing over my shoulder
with a heavy rain coming.

I remember a palm tree
blowing near the seashore.
People shouting with excitement
and their children too.

I remember me as a baby,
a little child screaming
'I need my milk and dinner,
otherwise I won't stop.'

I remember my new class,
as strange as a bumble bee,
Butterflies everywhere
near my knee.

I remember a new rainbow appearing,
Jesus brought it really near.
Jesus brought the land and the seas
and especially the world.

I remember some special Jesus
and his disciples,
all bring love and care.

I remember me walking past a little, pretty farmyard
with my big red wellies on
in deep brown mud.
I sang 'I like this poem very much.'

Adele Morgan (9)
St Joseph's RC Primary School, Aylesham

My Perfect Day

First Peter Andre took me to the park
And then we headed home when it got dark.

Me and All Saints partied all night
Whilst Scary and Ginger had a mean 'n' nasty pillow fight.

Taylor and I danced the night away
Sash came round and decided to stay.

And I shared some ice-cream with Vanilla
While Gary Barlow wrestled with a gorilla.

Aqua and me swam under the sea
And even 911 popped round for tea.

Isaac Hanson was playing with his Lego
Ant and Dec slipped on some yellow snow.

Shola Ama sang 'You might need Somebody'
Nick Backstreet Boys came to call on me.

Natalie Imbreugulia's pants got torn
Kavana went to mow the lawn.

The Teletubbies came round for Tubby Custard
Zac Hanson washed his hair with mustard.

My day I confess did not seem like a dream
But when I woke, I thought 'Ain't life mean'.

Natalie Johnstone (8)
St Joseph's RC Primary School, Aylesham

TALK TO ME

Talk to me
Holly tree
About your sharp little prickles
Or about your poor shiny red berries.

Talk to me
Holly leaves
About your life
Tell me about your strife
When the wind comes whistling through.

Tell me
Little happy likeable holly berry
What do you feel like when
Those naughty little birds
Eat your poor helpless holly berry friends.
Defeated?
Maybe so.
But right now I'm going home for tea.

Carla Petch (9)
St Joseph's RC Primary School, Aylesham

SEA

The ship sails the sea
Swish, the waves splash
The waves crash the boat
Splashing and crashing
There's a sunset shining along the sea
The sunset has gone far beneath and
All that's left is a dark and crisp shine.

Laura Picarelli (9)
St Joseph's RC Primary School, Aylesham

DAN THE FLINGMAN

I am Dan the Flingman
Catch me, catch me.
You can run over a house
and over a crane
and over a bridge
and over a train
and over flowers
and over trees
and over mountains
and Scottish sea.
I am Dan the Flingman
Catch me, catch me
if you can.
All the people ran and ran.
They caught Dan the Flingman.

Latayah Bennett Hall (8)
St Joseph's RC Primary School, Aylesham

LAZY LIONS

A leapy lazy lion
Lazes across a bendy crinkly log.
A leapy lazy lion
Lies quietly in long crinkly crazy grass
As quietly as a mouse.
A lazy lion purrs
Like a cat
Then pounces.

Liam Thornton (9)
St Joseph's RC Primary School, Aylesham

CATS

Cats sleep
Anywhere
Any table
Any chair
Very furry
Very purry

Cats sleep
Anywhere
Top of a patio
Anyone's lap will do
Curling up in the day
Searching in the night.

Emma-Leigh Edwards (9)
St Joseph's RC Primary School, Aylesham

THE SHIP

The waves crashing against the ragged rocks
And the gulls flying and crying.
The ship crashing against the waves
And the waves whooshing over the ship.
The slaves working very hard
And all the rich men playing cards.
The sun setting in the sky
Smoothly and softly.

Christopher Campbell (8)
St Joseph's RC Primary School, Aylesham

QUICKLY

Quickly, Formula 1 comes round the corner,
Quickly, quickly the cheetah runs.
Quickly, quickly, quickly the whirlwind twirls round.
But quickest of all, thrust breaks the sound barrier.

Oliver Latham (9)
St Peter's Primary School, Canterbury

SHARK

Look, what's that shadow in the water?
It's very dark.
It's opened its mouth.
It's a shark!

Nicholas Blown (9)
St Peter's Primary School, Canterbury

FOOD

Ice-cream is yummy
Chocolate chip is very nice
Fizzy pop is sweet.

Hannah Loughran (9)
St Peter's Primary School, Canterbury

Crossly

Crossly the wind blows me around.
Crossly the mouse bit the cat.
Crossly the cat bit the dog.
Crossly the sea wrecked a ship.
Crossly the clouds threw thunderbolts.

Megan Logan (8)
St Peter's Primary School, Canterbury

Spring

Spring, spring coming here.
Yellow, red, blue flowers are growing.
Spring, spring coming here.
Making kids joyful.
Kids are having fun in the sun.

Morgana Lines (9)
St Peter's Primary School, Canterbury

Bubbles

Bubbles bubbles in the air
Bubbles bubbles everywhere.
Bubbles big and bubbles small
Bubbles floating, bubbles fall.

Isabelle Nash (9)
St Peter's Primary School, Canterbury

Doom

A hurricane is coming to town
Quick get underground
Ha ha! Doom will come upon this town
Time for me to plant your doom
I'll *destroy* everything in this town
Boom smash *doom!*

Oscar Thornton (9)
St Peter's Primary School, Canterbury

I Want To Paint

I want to paint the sky and sun, stars and the moon.
I want to paint the cliffs and the beach.
I want to paint my page bright green.
I want to paint my room bright pink.
I want to paint my brother blue
and turn him into something new.

Catherine Walsh (8)
St Peter's Primary School, Canterbury

Spring

S pring is waking lots of animals.
P etals are on the flowers.
R ain is rarely coming.
I listen to the birds singing their songs.
N ew lambs are born.
G oing in the garden to look for animals.

Jake Upward (9)
St Peter's Primary School, Canterbury

I Want

I want to dream
I am driving a racing car
Going around a track.
I want to dream
I am in a tournament
Driving really fast.
I hope my dream comes true.

Nathan Hoare (9)
St Peter's Primary School, Canterbury

Autumn

A utumn is a time for the leaves to fall off
U can play in puddles
T he leaves go red and they fall off the trees
U can play with conkers
M oony nights are bright
N o more, no more leaves on the trees.

Peter Sakwa (9)
St Peter's Primary School, Canterbury

Spring

Pale flowers on the grass
Start to grow as the days pass.
People playing in the sun
Running around and having fun.
Flowers growing day after day
My dogs can go outside and play.

Lucy Harding (9)
St Peter's Primary School, Canterbury

My Mixture

I want to paint the sky and the clouds
and the biggest tree.

I want to be a monkey swinging from tree to tree
I'd like to be a whale roaming the sea.

I want to meet Lara Croft to see how she isn't scared,
and how she holds her breath for so long,
the way she tackles the wolves, bears and bats.

I want to draw something wacky, wild and weird,
I want to draw a cartoon theme.

I want to dream of a dragon flying, a crocodile swimming,
a dog with a gun, a kangaroo sitting on the loo
and a madman in a zoo.

William Parnall (9)
St Peter's Primary School, Canterbury

Hopefully

Hopefully I will do my work.
Hopefully it will be Xmas soon.
Hopefully I will go to bed at 8.00.
Hopefully I will get you up at 7.00.
Hopefully my dad will come back home.
Hopefully the clock is right.
Hopefully I will go to school.

Hannah Barker (9)
St Peter's Primary School, Canterbury

Bubbles

Bubbles big bubbles small,
Bubbles pop when they fall.
Bubbles here bubbles there,
Bubbles nearly everywhere.
Bubbles bubbles in the grass,
Bubbles bubbles really fast.
Bubbles bubbles fly up high,
Bubbles bubbles in the sky.
Bubbles bubbles you're so light,
Bubbles bubbles you get a free flight.
Bubbles bubbles stop stop stop!
Bubbles bubbles you're going to pop!
Bubbles bubbles you are so high,
We can't catch you, so goodbye!

Harry Parkin (8)
St Peter's Primary School, Canterbury

Spring

In spring the days get longer
and the flowers grow.

In spring the lambs are born
and the weather changes.

In spring hedgerows come out
and it is Easter.

Jodie Corrigan (8)
St Peter's Primary School, Canterbury

Creepy Crawly

Creepy crawly in the bath
Waiting to spring out on me.
Creepy crawly in the cellar
Going to scare me even if I hide.
Creepy crawly in the garden
Looking at me in the eye.
Creepy crawly in my bed
Tickling me, I'm scared.
Creepy crawly in the morning
Creepy crawly where is he?
Creepy crawly there he is,
He's lying down, oh no he's dead.

Anna Hamilton (9)
St Peter's Primary School, Canterbury

I Live In An Electronic Car

I live in a fast electronic car.
A mad, fast, electronic car.
It skids off the table
And into the baby's cradle.
I live in a fast electronic car.
A mad, fast, electronic car!

On the outside it's red and yellow.
On the outside it's got wires coloured.
Red, blue and yellow!
I live in a fast electronic car.
A mad, fast, electronic car!

Patrick Boal (9)
St Peter's Primary School, Canterbury

Spring

Spring is the time of year when new life is very near.
Plants are coming out high,
Trying to stretch and hit the sky.
Right at the start of spring,
All the birds start to sing.
In the night,
In the spring,
You can see everything.
Night has fallen in the sky,
Moths are hunted way up high.
Growing plants are here,
And remember, new life is always near.

Daniel Sherman (9)
St Peter's Primary School, Canterbury

An Autumn Scene

The golden haze across the sky as rusted leaves go by.
The smell of warm oak fills the air.
Across the pond sits the Grange.
The air is dark and the cool night draws on.
The rain falls.
I'm away from the Grange in the street.
It's cold and the lights are on.

As I wake up, the golden haze is back again.
The trees sway in the cool winds and lose the last few leaves they have.
The floor is a mass of dusted red and golden leaves.
In the back at the Grange, everywhere is damp.
Black ice is in front of the Grange.
Slippery and hidden.

Hannah Cheesley (10)
Saltwood CE Aided Primary School

Volcano

A lake of lava rushing down,
Spurts of magma
Glowing bombs crashing,
Sea spray, whirling onto the rocks
Destroying things in its path,
Bubbles are coming to the surface,
Steaming clouds of ash
Rise to the air,
Lava, rocks and stones burning life around it,
Few escape the spitting of the volcano's breath.

Lily Kendall (8)
Saltwood CE Aided Primary School

Volcano

Rumbling volcano,
Hot and smoking,
Bubbling and exploding,
Killing - then creating!
New islands
For iguanas and animals,
Orange bright lava,
Animals murdered - or surviving!

Alex Simons (8)
Saltwood CE Aided Primary School

Volcano

Swirling
Lava flows down the side of the volcano,
As it does,
It sparkles like bright stars,
It trickles down like syrup,
Flows into the sea,
Like a race as it rushes,
The sea burns like fire.
The lava glistens as it melts into the sea.
Now the sea bubbles.

Katie Medlicott (8)
Saltwood CE Aided Primary School

New Bear

Nothing but new and brown
Eyes like a shining blue mountain.
Wailing and squeaking like a cat
Black paws shining like silk.
Ears as small as a fingernail
All soft and dark fur.
Rough nose but not as rough as the ground.
Soft, sweet and cuddly.

Eloise George (8)
Saltwood CE Aided Primary School

Volcano

Great streams of glowing lava
Rushing along,
Powerful lava bombs,
Shooting out like fireworks,
Spitting over the earth like
A giant's little boy.
Blazing over the creatures,
Some are lucky,
Some are not!

Lucy Hurley (8)
Saltwood CE Aided Primary School

Cosmic

On a clear, starry night, in the loneliness of space,
Streamline jets zooming, through the glittering night sky.
Nuclear missiles burn their way through the atmosphere,
Into a huge swarm of stars.
Sailing through the universe,
A huge meteor lights the signal.
As the ballistic rockets crash towards the immense earth,
A faint star becomes a black hole.
When the missiles hit the ground,
the huge meteor bursts into the sulphur-surfaced sun.
As the radioactive clouds sweep across the earth,
Debris builds up in the asteroid belt.
On a clear, starry night, in the loneliness of space,
The supersonic jets steer homeward, through the glittering night sky.

Christopher Hannan
Sandown CP School

Cosmic

Cosmic dust floating through space.
Rockets swooping through the dark spacey air.
Meteorites getting hotter and hotter as they get closer to the sun.
Black holes suddenly appearing in space,
as it sucks the planets going through its dark, dark mouth.
Satellites slowly going through space, around earth.

Alex Riley (8)
Sandown CP School

Stars

Stars burst like a firework
Glittery, sparkling, fantastic
Shining, twinkling
Beautiful, lovely colours
Silvery, like glitter.

Oliver Arendell (5)
Sandown CP School

Stars

Stars are fantastic, like glitter.
They burst like fireworks.
Stars are silver.
They twinkle and sparkle.

Melissa Young (6)
Sandown CP School

Cosmic

A space port in space.
Jupiter and Mars on their way.
So many stars like balls full of gas.
Rockets zooming past the sun.
Imagine living inside a space city!
Imagine all the stars turning black . . .

Timothy Pitcher (8)
Sandown CP School

A Year Of Exploration In Space

Deep in the darkness of space,
The rarest sight of all,
The world's greatest fantasy about to come to life.
Sorrow as you think of family and friends,
To hover in mid air,
Shock when you hear we might not make it,
Gladness when you return to Earth.

Connie Turner (9)
Sandown CP School

Cosmic

Stars are twinkling in the sky
Rockets blowing planet to planet
Earth is like a ball, rolling round
Earth is like an apple
Stars are like tin-foil, shining in the sky
Rockets swoop round the moon.

Vicky Smith (8)
Sandown CP School

The Second Neil Armstrong

As we flew around in space,
I saw the most spectacular thing.
It made history,
It was earth's second moon.
We landed right on it
And planted the flag.
I didn't know what to expect
When we landed back on earth.
I felt like the second Neil Armstrong.
I hope to go again one day,
To see planet Earth's flag.

Ben Marshall (9)
Sandown CP School

Cosmic

Out in the dark dark galaxy
in my rocket I shoot to Mars.
I see the stars
while they twinkle in my eye.
Everything weighs less on the moon,
it is like walking on air.
The earth is like a dot,
waiting for the people to come back.

Emma Lawless (8)
Sandown CP School

SPACE

Waiting quietly, nervous and scared,
excited but anxious, sitting in the chair.
Suddenly we zoomed so high, I prayed.

I'm seeing the earth as a quiet place
with white fluffy clouds,
all over the place.

I'm walking on Pluto, Venus and Mars,
none of them with life.
All I can see is earth and the stars.

Jasmin Douglas (9)
Sandown CP School

SPACE

Spaceships flying in space,
Zooming through the cosmic atmosphere.
Planets never seen,
UFOs shooting by.
Stars sparkling in space,
Meteorites striking the ground,
Asteroids flowing in a belt,
Amazing comets pass.

Luke Friend (8)
Sandown CP School

GLITTERING VENUS

I got into my space shuttle.
I shut the door and counted down
5, 4, 3, 2, 1, blast off.
I was going up really fast.
I was proud but a bit scared at first.
At last I got to Venus.
It glittered and dazzled.
It looked like someone had sprinkled glitter over it.
Maybe I was not scared anymore.
I felt very happy that I had come after all.

Alison Borg (9)
Sandown CP School

COSMIC

Stars twinkling at night
Colourful and silvery.
They're fantastic
They burst like a firework.
They stay in the sky
And they shoot across the sky.
Some of them stay in place.
They're sparkling at night.
They shine in the sky at night.

Charlotte Lavender (6)
Sandown CP School

Cosmic

In space it is great,
It twinkles, it sparkles too.
Oh, it's great to be in space.
See the rocket zooming by.
All the stars are smiling as I go by.
See it as you go by.
The moon is lovely when it's winking at me.
There's Pluto, it's bumpy and lumpy.
See Earth spinning round.
See the sun shining at me in the morning.

Laura Arendell (7)
Sandown CP School

Cosmic

One big spaceship with a fiery tail twirling
through the stars and moon *zoom!*
Zooming through the mysterious space and past Mars,
Past a comet and landed on Pluto with a bump.
Steamy, bumpy craters too.
Suddenly it took off and started floating in space.
It got hotter and hotter as it go nearer to the sun.
Suddenly a comet nearly hit
One big spaceship with a fiery tail twirling through the stars.

Jessica Shiel (8)
Sandown CP School

Crocodile Teeth

Crocodile teeth are sometimes yellow,
Because they've been having fish,
Fish for tea, fish for lunch,
I think it's their favourite dish.

Crocodile teeth are sometimes yellow,
But now I have to explore,
The crocodile is brushing its teeth I'm afraid,
He seems to have eaten class 4.

Crocodile teeth are sometimes yellow,
I've seen some and a skull too,
I saw some crocodiles in a bush,
And then ran. Yahoo!

Crocodile teeth are sometimes yellow,
I ran all the way to the sea,
The crocodile is brushing his teeth I'm afraid,
I think he's going to eat me!

Ian Merrick (9)
Sandwich Junior School

At School

At school I play in the playground.
At school I paint in the classroom.
At school in the classroom I work.
In the playground I sing.
In the playground I sit in the quiet area.

Amanda Shirley (9)
Sandwich Junior School

GUIDO FAWKES NIGHT

Bang! Kaboom!
Guido's burnt soon.
Kerang! Fizz!
The Catherine wheel goes whiz.
Sizzle! Clang!
The rocket goes bang.
Whiz! Whoosh!
Don't push in front of the fire or they'll join Guido.

The final fireworks go off,

Suddenly silence. Everyone's gone home.
Time to put
the fire *out!*

Daniel Clayton (9)
Sandwich Junior School

WHEN I STEP INTO THE PICTURE

When I step into the picture,
I see a man on a horse.
I see a man on a boat.
The boat has just come from the castle.
There was lots of people coming towards me,
So I step out of the picture.

James Chapman (9)
Sandwich Junior School

FIREWORKS

A Million rockets leave the sky,
exploding to make a pretty sight.

A Catherine wheel spins just like a,
colourful plate stuck on a stick

No screamers scream as loud as me,
but they travel far up in the sky fast

Orange and yellow flames dart out,
of the fire furiously as I watch

Guys burn down as the fireworks display ends.

Daniel Evans (9)
Sandwich Junior School

MY BOX OF DREAMS

In my box of dreams
I'm a famous footballer called Ryan Giggs.
I'm a pop star called Baby Spice.
I'm the king of France.
I'm at the Olympics doing a dance.
I'm on television with Michael Barrymore.
But when I shut the lid of my box of dreams
Then I'm just me.

Kirsty Jones (9)
Sandwich Junior School

AUTUMN

The leaves are back!
The golden red ones you mean.
'Yes' I reply with a noisy wallop for the tree.
The shimmering leaves crunch as they fall
down, down, down.
The wind goes whoosh and blows the leaves away.
The rain falls . . .
Pitter, patter, pitter, patter
and faster
and faster!
then it stopped.

Hattie Perkins (9)
Sandwich Junior School

TEDDY BEARS

There are all kinds of teddy bears,
Big ones and small.
I don't have a favourite, I like them all.
Some with tails, some with ears.
There are all kinds of teddy bears.

Yellow, blue and green bears.
Some with noses, some with clothes.
I have a teddy called Teddy Toes
Yellow, blue and green bears.

Amy van Poppel (9)
Sandwich Junior School

Sad, Lost And Lonely

My cat has gone
sad,
lost
and
lonely
And never returned
sad,
lost
and
lonely
We look for him at night
sad,
lost
and
lonely
But he never came back
sad,
lost
and
lonely
But we found him today
not sad,
lost
nor
lonely.

Lorrianne Davis (9)
Southborough Primary School

My Dog

I have a dog named Jessie
sometimes she's rather messy.

She comes in from outside
with mud on her paws
and wipes it all over the floor.

She jumps up on my bed
and curls up by my head
and sometimes she even snores.

She prefers to be outdoors.
We take her up the woods.
She loves to play with sticks
She does some very clever tricks.

We race around the trees
and try not to hurt our knees.
We play hide and seek
and try not to sneeze.

We took her to a race,
she nearly bit someone's face.
We came home with a prize,
it brought tears to my eyes.
I really hope she never dies.

Martin Baker (9)
Southborough Primary School

TEDDY

T eddy bear fell asleep
E ating his honey
D anger at night
D anger at day
Y elling 'Help, help I am all sticky.'

Steven Theaker (8)
Southborough Primary School

TEDDY

T wo dangling legs
E ach one has pads
D oes he walk for miles?
D ucking under a fence.
Y ou have found the teddy.

Blake Brett (8)
Southborough Primary School

BEARS

B ears, soft and cute
E ars, big ears, small
A nimals they are
R ound and round, they go far.

Craig Morley (8)
Southborough Primary School

Dance Of The Dolphins

Slow, slow, quick, quick, slow,
ride the waves
and here we go.

Quick, quick, leap up high,
arch your back,
it's time to fly.

Fly, fly, puff and blow,
blow some bubbles
in a row.

Puff, puff, waltz and spin,
shake your tail,
flick your fin.

Slow, slow, quick, quick, slow,
take a partner,
dive down low.

Quick, quick, slow, slow, quick,
listen carefully,
that's the trick!

Bethany Sturtivant (9)
Southborough Primary School

Chocolate

1 for the Mars
2 for the Twix
3 to get it ready now go, go, go
but don't you eat my Milky Way.
You can do anything but eat my Milky Way.

Carl Tanton (8)
Southborough Primary School

A Teddy Bear Poem

Teddy bears are cuddly
Even when they're old
I cuddle mine at night
Even though I'm eight years old
He helps me when there is a fright
By holding me really tight.

Charlotte Marchant (8)
Southborough Primary School

The Kite

Flying high, flying low,
Doesn't really know
Which way to go
It flies round here
It flies round there
Lots of people stop and stare.

Bradley Murphy (8)
Southborough Primary School

Kites

The most amazing thing about kites
is they come in these giant sizes,
and any colour you fancy.
Most fly in the sky
But mine flies on the ground.

Mishelle Wallace (8)
Southborough Primary School

My Cat Max

Max is my cat,
He's black and fat.
He sleeps all day,
That's his way.
My cat's name is Max,
He loves to relax.
He likes his food,
He's a handsome, cool dude.
He's got a friend called Fig,
Who's not very big.
They play and fight,
All day and night.
He goes out at night,
Looking for a fight.
He comes in in the morning,
As the rain is pouring.
He sits by the fire,
Where he gets drier.

Jade Parkin (8)
Southborough Primary School

My Favourite Bird

Flies at night,
catches in flight.
But makes a great sight,
Stuns its prey,
then flies away.
What likes to prowl,
my friend the owl.

Adam Lott (9)
Southborough Primary School

The Seasons

Spring is when the flowers grow.
Spring is when it rains.
Spring is when the lambs are born
and the cricket starts again.

Summer's when it's very hot.
It's when the sun shines bright
In the holidays we go to the beach
and have barbecues at night.

Autumn's the time the leaves turn brown.
We plant bulbs for spring.
The horse chestnut gives us conkers
and the harvest gifts we bring.

Christmas comes in wintertime.
Sometimes we get snow.
We run around playing football
and we keep our fires aglow.

Matthew Parrish (8)
Southborough Primary School

Football Crazy

It's football mad, it's football crazy
everybody's going insane.
The sun is shining on the pitch.
The birds are singing in the trees
and now the match begins.
The first goal by Ryan Giggs.
The Reds have just defeated Chelsea
now they're all sad and alone.

Jason Bennett (8)
Southborough Primary School

A Friend

I once had a friend,
who was new to the school.
I once had a friend,
who the kids thought was cool.
I once had a friend,
who pushed me in the river.
I once had a friend,
who made me shiver.
I once had a friend,
who stole my packed lunch.
I once had a friend,
who gave me a punch.
I once had a friend
who would laugh when I fall.
So I guess he wasn't a friend,
at all.

Ysobel Hallett (9)
Southborough Primary School

Holidays

H appy smiles at play
O cean waves are small
L ighthouse we explore
I ce-creams are fun when they melt down your chin
D arker clouds come at night and so do bigger waves
A ction lightning flashes by
Y ellow sky in the morning
S o much fun are holidays.

Natalie Cole (8)
Southborough Primary School

Guess Who?

It is something for girls to go mad about.
To jump up and down and say they are gorgeous.
To not be able to sleep at night.
And not think about them all day.
All my friends love them as much as I do.
But the problem is.
What if they don't like me that much.
One of them is white.
One is tan.
They hang around the other girls.
But I love them just the same.
Well can you guess who they are?
My old and new ponies Albie and Fraggie.

Rebecca King (9)
Southborough Primary School

The Rescue At Sea

I see a beautiful dolphin in the sea,
splashing and swimming and diving with glee.
A shark is circling me, trying to bite me.
The dolphin swims nearer, help me, Oh please!

The dolphin hits the shark with her bottle-shaped nose,
I am so scared I shake from my head to my toes.
I will put up a sign so everyone knows
not to swim here, this is where the shark goes.

Hannah Perry (8)
Southborough Primary School

Teddy Bears

T oday I'll play with ted
E very day I'll play with him
D ressing him to go to bed
D roopy ted whose name is Jim
Y es this bear is the best.

B edtime teddy
E ars and arms that are so brown
A rms and legs that turn around
R ound and round it's time for bed
S o soft teddy 'Good night.'

Abbey Lant (9)
Southborough Primary School

Happy And Wild

She ran through the field,
happy and wild,
she kicked up the grass,
happy and wild,
she ate the grass,
happy and wild,
night falls and all is dark,
she ran through the field,
happy and wild.

Courtney Marie Dack (9)
Southborough Primary School

The Night Sky

A black sheet covers the earth's sky.
Glittering, shining, blinding stars,
Light up the blackness of the silent night.
The streets, dark, deserted, quiet,
Are only lit up by the great stars.
The green shaded trees stand just like stone statues.
Then suddenly lights burst through the pitch, black sky.
Then, some more light and more until the very first bird
Is singing its morning song.
Finally daybreak has come.

Joshua Marks (10)
Southborough Primary School

My Dog Jack

My dog Jack is short and fat
With a few spots on his back.

He has a brown head,
With a little brown bed,
and a snuggle made of patches.

He has a shiny nose
and little curly toes
and his tail just loves to wag.

Aimée Franklin (9)
Southborough Primary School

Teddy Bear

T eddy's always there
E very day, every night
D azzling eyes
D eep, dark eyes
Y ellow ribbon around its neck

B ig bears everywhere
E ars are furry
A rms, short and hard
R ound, fat belly.

Graham Voisey (9)
Southborough Primary School

The Cheeky Children

The cheeky children
Had some chocolate
For Christmas.
Later on that night
The cheeky children
Went out for a Chinese.
They chewed on
The chicken Chow Mein.
When the cheeky
Children got home
The cheeky children
Saw a chimpanzee.
The chimpanzee cheekily
Chuckled and chased them
Out of the door!

Stephen Harris & Luke Newman (8)
Teynham CP School

THE TIGER

The nose of the tiger,
Twitches with hunger,
The smell of prey,
Is close by,
The tiger creeps through the grass,
Like an uncertain tourist.

The tiger pounces,
For its prey,
The prey is fast,
But no match for the tiger.

The prey,
Is . . .
Is . . .
A mouse.

And no more will be said,
When the tiger is,
Dead.

Robert Ainsworth (9)
Teynham CP School

THE SLIMY SNAKE

There was a snake crawling through the garden.
It was green and slimy
It crawled around the bench and slid through the fence
And it ended up all grimy . . .

Alex Taylor & Anthony Kay (8)
Teynham CP School

PIGS

So fat,
So pink,
But what a terrible stink.
A little fat nose,
With trotters for toes.
Little black eyes
A tummy full of pies.

All day long they roll in the mud,
When they jump they land with a thud.
They don't wear boots,
Or any suits.
A tail so curly
It's nearly twirly.

Natalie Browning (9)
Teynham CP School

DINOSAURS

Dinosaurs are scaly,
Stegosaurus is spiky,
T-Rex stamping through the grass
Roaring on the way
Looking for its food,
Crunching all the bones.

Jack Deacon, Eoin Mehlin (7) & Charles Hammant (9)
Teynham CP School

My Brother

My little brother, Daniel
He runs around like mad.
He makes the house a pigsty
And wonders what to mess up next.

I have a brother called David,
He's up to the level to make him a devil
He pushes you around and you fall on the ground.
He makes you play at the end of the day.

I have a brother called Daniel,
He's such a nightmare to handle.
He swallowed a dog as thin as a log
And now he's a cocker spaniel.

Sophie Nason, Sally Ann Walters & Francesca Burgess (8)
Teynham CP School

My Favourite Animal

My favourite animal he's the best,
He's a gerbil and he's got a vest,
I've got a crocodile he's green and scary
When people see him they're always wary!
My favourite animal is a guinea-pig he's the best
He's the winner in the west, he's called Ginger
And everyone calls him a whinger.

Rebecca Tolhurst, Laura Lewis (8) & Hannah Elsey (9)
Teynham CP School

The Sea

Running on the sand
feet getting warm
and flying up high
a bees swarm.

In the sea
Waves crashing
on the sandy shore
water splashing.

Boats afloat
in the sea
What a glorious
place to be.

Rebecca Cooper (9)
Teynham CP School

One Windy Night

One night it was cold and windy.
The raindrops banged on the window.
Me and my friend were in at home,
With no one else in the house.
The door banged open.
Footsteps went up the stairs,
It was scary.

Emma Jane Lethbridge (9), Natalie
Jade Welsh (8) & Ryan Richards (9)
Teynham CP School

The Rainy Day

The rain falls down
On the ground.
Splash! Splash! Splash!
Blue rain.
White rain.
Pitter, patter, pitter, patter.
The rain falls down.
Splash! Splash! Splash!
On the ground.
Tat, tat, tat.
Ratter, tat, tat.

Sophie Washer (8)
Teynham CP School

The Rainy Day

Pitter, patter
The rain pours down
I am getting
Soaking wet.
Pitter, patter,
Ratter, tat, tat.
Let me in!
I'm soaking wet!

Emma Boorman (9)
Teynham CP School

The Earthquake

The earth shook
Roads were shook down.
There was crashing
Banging, everywhere.
Houses were falling,
Cars crashing,
People crying for help.
Buildings crashing
To the floor.
Everyone is sad.

Simon Hall (9)
Teynham CP School

Rocks

Black shimmering,
Rocks falling down.
The cliff falling
Into the sea
Out of sight
Forever gone.
Boom, smash, crash,
Into the deep
Deep sea.
Never to be seen again!

Stephen Lewis (9)
Teynham CP School

I'M SCARED

I'm scared of
Spiders
The black eight-legged
Arachnid
Am scared of
Bats
The animal who
Flies in the
Dark, dark
Night
Am scared of
Crocodiles
The animal who
Snaps his
Prey
Am scared of the
Great white shark
Who has
Mighty sharp
Teeth
Am scared of
Ghosts
Who go
Boo!

Emily Lamb (9)
Westborough CP School

Springtime Is Here

Spring is here again,
Children playing everywhere,
Laughter in the air,
Daffodils dancing,
Bluebells blooming,
Sunshine everywhere,
Grasshoppers hopping,
Frogs are jumping,
Tadpoles hatching everywhere,
Birds are chirping,
Trees are blossoming,
Spring is in the air,
Lighter evenings,
Picnics in the park,
It's holidays at last.
Buttercups and clover,
Lambs in the meadow,
Horses galloping,
Rabbits darting everywhere,
Pansies smiling in the sun.

Yvette Vinten (9)
Westborough CP School

On Sunday Noon

On Sunday noon I went to the moon
In a beautiful pea green rocket
I took millions of chocolates
And billions of money
And what a beautiful day it was!

Jessica Owens (9)
Westborough CP School

SUMMER

In the crops of golden corn
Where the poppies are all born
I lie and watch the sky

As the birds go flying by
I fall asleep into a dream
Float on a cloud where I'm not seen.

Holly Partridge (8)
Westborough CP School

SPOOKY GOINGS ON

Sometimes I think somebody is there
But it's just the wind whistling through my hair
But most of the time it's just me imagining things
And as the wind howls round my window, my sister
Shouts out 'There's something spooky going on
So just watch out.'

Kylie Cooper (9)
Westborough CP School

SUMMER DAY

Summer sun having fun
being very jolly.
Playing with my friend
all day
Eating an ice-cream lolly.

Lianne Crittenden (7)
Westborough CP School

I SAW

I saw a pink fire
I saw a pig fly
I saw a jumping toothbrush
I saw a dancing pie.

I saw the sun in the middle of the night
I saw a balloon made of steel
I saw a table run a race
I saw a square car wheel.

I saw a dog four hundred feet tall
I saw a penguin in a fight
I saw a cloud fall from the sky
I saw a peacock write.

I saw a cat jump four hundred feet high
I saw a shoe play golf
I saw a book turn a page on its own
I saw a flying bread loaf.

Michael Ingleton (9)
Westborough CP School

RAINFOREST

The rainforest is awake.
I hear the birds singing
as they sit on my branches every morning.
Sometimes I even hear the little babies
calling their mother for food.
I even see birds building their nests.
The little birds go cheep cheep cheep
and the big birds go toot toot toot.

Marie Lorimer (8)
Westborough CP School

If I Could Be Anything

If I could be anything I would be a cat,
Soft, fluffy, lazy and fat.
I'd sleep all day long on my owner's lap,
At night I'd go hunting out through my cat flap.
I'd catch voles for my supper,
A mouse for a snack,
A shrew as a gift to my owner which
I'd leave outside their bedroom door,
And then out again to play for just a little while more.
The sun comes up,
My playtime is done.
The night is over now and so is my fun.
I can lay sleeping all day,
In my comfortable warm house,
Peacefully dreaming of last night's prey,
The voles, the shrew and the mouse.

Kelly Johnston (9)
Westborough CP School

My Poem

As pretty as a flower,
As friendly as a cat,
As noisy as a dog,
You can't come cleverer than that.

As tall as a giraffe,
As bright as the sun,
As joyful as a clown,
That's as polite as they come.

Emma Walton (8)
Westborough CP School

I'M NOT FRIGHTENED OF LIFE

The dark, dark night,
The horrifying tomb,
The spooky graveyard,
I'm not frightened of life.

The giant hairy spider in the bath,
The spooky shadows in the dark,
The curving grey shark,
I'm not frightened of life.

The night of Hallowe'en,
The people who trick or treat me,
They scare me! Not really!
I'm scared of what?
Am I?
Nothing!

Jessica Dean (9)
Westborough CP School

AUTUMN

The wind
whistles through
the thistles the
wind blows through
the trees and sends
a big breeze.
The wind jumps over
the mountain and
bumps into the clouds.
And then it starts
all over again.
But really, really loud.

Katie Vaughan (7)
Westborough CP School

In My Perfect World

When I look through my window
I see
Soft chocolate
Like fluffy pillars
Slimy rivers
Like water in your mouth
Big hills
Like sweets.

Levi Draper (9)
West Malling CEP School

In My Perfect World

When I look through my window
I see
Mountainous trees
Like a humungous giant's yummy sweets
Like a blazing hot Mars bar
A muddy squashy floor
Like a bubbling chocolate pudding.

Katie Ashton (9)
West Malling CEP School

In My Perfect World

When I look through my window
I see glittering stars in the sky
I can see a perfect river flowing by
And sparkling I see beautiful stars
In the sky like diamonds.

Kerrie Gibbs (9)
West Malling CEP School

In My Perfect World

In my perfect world,
When I look through my window,
I see,
A stripy ice-cream stand
Like a dream,
Sticky lollies
Like ice when you touch it,
Little crabs
Like pebbles on the seashore,
Green palm trees
Like a crooked old man,
Fluffy candyfloss
Like a cuddly teddy bear,
Lovely shells
Like gems shining in the sand.

Emily Roalfe (8)
West Malling CEP School

In My Perfect World

When I look out my window
I see
A tree half money and half sweets
Like a caramel river
In a candy forest
With a sparkling sun
The sun is like
A yellow wrapper
In a blue sky.

Joshua Jiles (9)
West Malling CEP School

In My Perfect World

When I look through my window
I see
Long damp grass
Like a blanket of green
Buzzing bees
Like a lawnmower
A playing dog
Like a car going very fast
And a bird tweeting
Like someone singing
And trickling water
Like a tap.

Christopher Harris (8)
West Malling CEP School

In My Perfect World

In my perfect world
When I look through my window
I see
Melting chocolate stars
Like a milky river
A moon which lights up in the dark
Like white chocolate rain
Like diamonds dropping down
Enormous tall trees
Like long-necked giraffes.

Emma Harrison (8)
West Malling CEP School

In A Perfect World

In my perfect world
When I look through my window
I see
A hot baked sun
Like a beautiful ripened cake
Bright flowers growing
Like happily married people
And birds singing
Like flutes playing wildly
With large and tiny animals
Running mad.

Sam Wall (10)
West Malling CEP School

Weather

Weather can be hot, cold and windy
Sometimes it is raining, thundering, sunny
It is burning in the morning, freezing later on.
I wish weather would make up its mind
When I start skipping the wind comes over
Then I come out of lunch, it is cold.
As soon as I am in school it is warm.
I wish weather would make up its mind.
When I have fun it is chilly.
If I am not it is sizzling.
Weather can be annoying,
Look at all the things that it does,
Weather is hot, cold, warm, rainy and sunny
And tomorrow will be a better day!

Abinaya Selladurai (8)
Westgate CP School

DOLPHINS

Dolphins I like
They leap out the waves at night
They attack sharks when they attack you
They are quite harmless
And should be your friend.

Dolphins I like
They leap out the waves at night
If they are not your friend
Then make them soon
Or they won't like you.

Dolphins I like
They leap out the waves at night
They can be tame and turned into your pets
They can do tricks
And jump through hoops
That's why I like them so much!

Dolphins I like
They leap out the waves at night
They are a bit like whales
But a bit smaller and dainty
So they can jump out the waves at night!

Cheryl Barlow (8)
Westgate CP School

Love

Hearts beating together
Two people joined forever
Presents for him
Gifts for her
Surprises for them both
A ring of gold
A kiss for him
Some love for her.

Stacey Bassett (8)
Westgate CP School

My Cousin Jim

My cousin's name is Jim,
He really is quite dim.
Jim fights and knocks me over,
I set my dog on him, called Rover.
My mum gets cross with both of us,
So we make friends and go off on the bus.

Balraj Khunkhuna (9)
Westgate CP School

Snake

Snake,
Savage, slimy,
Slithering, slow, striking,
Scary,
Help!

Luke Prescott (9)
Westgate CP School

My Mum

My mum makes me eat peas,
It's not fair,
My mum takes me shopping,
It's not fair,
My mum makes me go to bed early,
It's not fair,
My mum makes me eat meat,
It's not fair,
My mum doesn't let me play out,
It's not fair,
My mum makes me eat toffees,
It's not fair,
I wonder if I'll be not fair when I'm older,
I hope not.

Charlotte Morris (9)
Westgate CP School

School

I go to school every day
It's really, really fun.
My teacher's called Miss Lomax
And my work's all done.
I'm going out to play now,
To play with all my friends
And when the school bell goes
Play is at an end.

Charlotte Porter (9)
Westgate CP School

Simple Simon

Simple Simon
Told the fireman
That his house
Was on fire

Simple Simon
Told the police
That where he lived
There was no peace

Simple Simon
Told the doctor
That he had the flu
But all this the doctor knew.

Hala Hosny (9)
Westgate CP School

The Leopard

The leopard awaits in the long grass
A herd of wildebeest come along
There is a baby one
'Let's go and have some fun.'
She crept closer and closer
Until she leapt
With a flash of her jaw the wildebeest was dead
And the leopard had a lovely feast.

Tamsin Etheridge (8)
Westgate CP School

FLOWERS

Flowers, flowers 1, 2, 3
Here comes Mr Bumble Bee
Pollen waiting for him to take
Lovely honey for him to make.

Flowers, flowers 4, 5, 6
Laying their heads upon the sticks
Petals red, yellow, blue,
Here are the flowers for me and you.

Flowers, flowers 7, 8, 9
This can be a proper rhyme
Flowers growing in their place
Puts a smile on everyone's face.

Charlotte Dale (8)
Westgate CP School

IT'S WET

It's wet, it's wet,
It's raining hard
Splash, splosh in the puddles
Flash, bang it's a storm.

First the lightning
Then the thunder
See the rain dancing
Pitter, patter on the window-pane.

Gurpreet Philora (9)
Westgate CP School

Dartford Town

Dartford town is very busy,
Sometimes it even makes me dizzy.
A lot of the time I meet some friends,
While I'm turning around the bends.

There are lots of shops in Dartford town,
But it never seems to get me down.
A lot of cars go through there,
But a few people just seem to stare.

Thursdays and on Saturdays too,
Sees a market, just for you!
Clothes, shoes, tapes and CDs,
All sorts of things - but nothing's for free.

Richard Mark Darby (8)
Westgate CP School

Goss Hawkes

It is a very faithful bird,
It also loves to talk,
It lives on all the hillsides,
And it has a funny walk.

It is quite lively,
It sings very sweetly,
But it is very deadly,
And it loves to live in Scotland.

Hannah Kirby (9)
Westgate CP School

Ghost

Ghosts are scary,
Ghosts come at night
Ghosts go under your bed
And give you a fright.

Ghosts are scary,
Ghosts are white,
Ghosts make loud noises,
And give you a fright.

Ghosts are friendly,
Ghosts are bright,
Ghosts are young and old,
And give you a fright.

Hayley Skiddy (9)
Westgate CP School

My Brother

I've got a brother
Rowan is his name
He goes to the park
Then he runs down the lane.
He's sometimes really naughty
But sometimes rather nice
His favourite food is rice.
Yes I've got a brother
And Rowan is his name.

Farran Wilkins (8)
Westgate CP School

CHINESE NEW YEAR

Fire crackers banging
Dragons swaying
People dancing
Drum bands playing
Lucky envelopes hanging up
Children drinking with a cup
Dragons doing the lion dance
People watching tigers prance
Lions jumping in the air
Oh what a lovely time to share
Decorations red and gold
In with the New Year out with the old.

Andrew Clark (8)
Westgate CP School

MY SCHOOL

My school is called Westgate,
There I see my best mates.
My favourite thing to do is writing,
And that is very exciting.
I go to school to learn,
House points are to earn.
I wear school uniform,
It makes you look smart,
And when I have the time,
I like to do art.

Palvinder Philora (8)
Westgate CP School

THE FROZEN MAN

One cold and frosty night
The moon shone like a
Big light
Then down on a hill
A man was stiff and a
Little shaky.
We thought
He might be lonely but our
Mum and Dad said, *no, no*.
It's too frosty to go out.
He is wearing a very thick hat
And a very soft pair of gloves.
All that he could see
Around him were trees
And fields of cows.
He was walking very slowly through
A great big open road.
He feels like he is going to sneeze
He was all alone so he stopped off at a
House where children sleep in a nice warm bed.
So he knocked
On the door.
'Come in, come in,' said Dad.
When he saw the house he
Was very warm already.
They got him a warm cup of cocoa
And a bed near the fire
So he wasn't cold or frosty anymore.

Kirsty Jane Harris (8)
Whitstable County Junior School

FIREWORKS

Whizzing, fizzing, pop, bang,
I hear fireworks,
Rockets screaming,
A big bonfire glowing red,
A water-fountain in all colours, red, green,
Orange and violet.
A great display this is.
A Catherine wheel spinning round and round.
Another big bang, it is a rocket.
Sausages for free.
Oooh, a big gliding banger just went up,
Scream, pop, the jumping jack just jumped at me.
It's like a dream, I start to fall asleep.
Bang that woke me up.
Fizz, whiz, it is traffic lights, green, red and orange.
It is time to go, *no, no.*
OK just for a little while,
Bang, whoosh, pop fizz.
A big screamer went up,
I love fireworks.

Rebecca Ball (9)
Whitstable County Junior School

FIREWORKS NIGHT

Fireworks night whizzing, popping, banging.
Jumping jack jumps over my head.
A whizzing rocket screams through the sky.
The fireworks whizz, turn, scream, bang.
The sausages sizzle, the fireworks bang.
The bonfire glows and then the guy is put on.
At the end I go home and dream of fireworks.

Reece Barratt (9)
Whitstable County Junior School

The Frozen Man

The frozen man is walking slowly down the road, frozen stiff,
so he can hardly move.
The moon shines in his face as he walks through the icy air.
He is all alone as he sits down on the kerb.
Leaves are falling down as he walks over to my house.
He knocks on my door.
I open the door for the man
to come through the warm touch of the house.
He is shivering as he goes in.
I asked the man if he would like a cup of tea.
He puts his hand near the fire as I come in
with the cup of tea.
I offered him a blanket - the man said no.
I shivered as he said no.
I asked him if he wanted a biscuit to eat,
he said yes.
I brought some cookies in for us!
He felt the boiling air as he picked up his cup of tea and drank.

Luke Moss (9)
Whitstable County Junior School

Autumn Mix

Mouldy apples laying on the ground,
lots of wheat so gold and round.
The leaves turn colours, brown and red,
as a hedgehog looks to find a bed.
As a bird stops to eat a berry,
children sound so very merry.
The air seems so crisp and clear,
because winter now is very near.

Alice Rose Dale (9)
Whitstable County Junior School

The Frozen Man

A frozen man
walks down a black, dark road.
The moon is shining in the dark.
He was wearing very thin gloves,
shivering to death,
he looks in people's windows
wishing he was there too.
Walking very slowly,
the frozen man trips over the snow
hoping that someone will let him in.
Then a lady comes out and lets him in.
She gives him some hot chocolate and biscuits.
The lady lets him stay overnight.
He was next to the fire.
When he had watched some TV,
he fell asleep.

Sam Bradford (9)
Whitstable County Junior School

The Frozen Man

The man is walking in the park.
He is wearing a thick blue top and his scarf is
wrapped around his neck.
It is a frosty early morning.
He runs towards a house and knocks on the door.
He goes inside and sees the fire all gold and red.
So he warms himself by it.
Someone gives him a mug of hot chocolate
and he drinks it down.
He is home.

Emma Rigden (9)
Whitstable County Junior School

The River

When winter came and froze the river
It was very cold and it made me quiver.
The poor ducks are sliding about,
I'm getting even colder so I've started to shout.
It doesn't seem to move but it's moving under ice.

I came back in the spring and a duck had broke his wing,
I gave him some bread but he threw it on my head,
So I gave him some cake instead.

I came back in the summer and found he wasn't there,
I got so sad and lonely,
I was pulling out my hair.

I went back in the autumn and I found him lying there,
I felt like I could touch him but I didn't even dare.

Emily Snellgrove (9)
Whitstable County Junior School

The Frozen Man

Wind, wind very cold,
The man needs some warmth.
The man's nose was red,
He was freezing cold like ice.
He didn't have any coat to wear,
Then he couldn't walk
Anywhere.
So he crawled when he found a house,
He knocked the door but no one was in the house.
But he went inside the house,
Then the wind went away as he wished.
Now he can play.

Tahnaz Hannan (8)
Whitstable County Junior School

Fireworks Night

Flashing, banging, shimmering gold,
Fireworks to behold.
Bending, twirling through the air,
A Catherine wheel is spinning there.
Sparklers crackling,
Children cackle,
One of them got too near, I'm sad to say
He's not here.
Take care,
Beware,
Beware,
Fireworks are dangerous,
Beware,
Beware.

Joseph Ferris-Moore (8)
Whitstable County Junior School

The Candyman

I am the writing on the wall
The whisper in the classroom
I am the candyman!
Some people know me as gum-chewer
Some people know me as a bee
Some people know me as the candyman
But I know myself as me!

Robert Willy (9)
Whitstable Endowed CE Junior School

PEACEFUL SAILING

The light clear sky high above
The deep blue sea down below,
The bobbing of the little boat,
How peaceful.

The birds are singing in the trees,
The wind bringing a gentle breeze,
The seagulls screeching in the sky,
How peaceful.

The wind is changing,
I'm sailing home,
The sun setting in the sky
How peaceful.

Lauren Knowles (9)
Whitstable Endowed CE Junior School

SCHOOL!

I like school!
School is fun.
At playtime I
play in the sun!

When lunchtime comes
I eat my plums
and feel very happy!

The bell goes,
and we put up our chairs!
Then we say our prayers!

Laura Siminson (9)
Whitstable Endowed CE Junior School

My Rabbits

I have two little rabbits sitting on the lawn.
They came to live with me, just after they were born.
They both have floppy ears, one is brown and one is black,
I call the first one Sooty and other I call Jack.
They feed on oats and cabbage, they like a drink as well,
I have to clean them weekly or else they start to smell.
At night they're in the garage, in the garden for the day,
We have to keep watch over, they don't bark like a puppy,
Or sing like a little bird, they let me know they like me
Without a spoken word.
So of all the little pets in north, south, east and west,
I love my little bunnies,
The dearest and the best.

Hannah Robinson (9)
Whitstable Endowed CE Junior School

Loneliness

I sit and wait by the telephone thinking
Why doesn't someone phone me up and invite me to their house?
Why do I have to be alone?
How can I make someone be my friend?
Why don't I have someone to talk to who can understand?
Why when we pick teams am I always the last to be chosen?
Why?
Do I look like an alien?
Do I mess about?
Do people think I'm a bully?
Please tell me.
Give me a shout.

Kate Blamires
Wincheap Junior GM School

THE WITCH'S BREW

Into the pot there now must go,
A skeleton's foot and
A fox's toe.

Hubble, bubble at the double
Cooking pot stir up some trouble,
My old grandma's ring
And my best party dress
Six chopped pumpkins, what a mess!

Hubble, bubble at the double
Cooking pot stir up some trouble.
My mother's wig
A heart of a pig
A dead bull's horn
A T-shirt that's torn.

Hubble, bubble at the double
Cooking pot stir up some trouble
A tongue of a lizard
A foot of a crow
Two bats' wings
And all the colours of the rainbow.

Hubble, bubble at the double
Cooking pot stir up some trouble.

Laura Riding & Amy Gibbs (9)
Wincheap Junior GM School

A Smile For The World

I'm looking in the mirror,
who do I see, a small nose and long blond hair,
two blue eyes looking most aware,
two rosy cheeks and little pink lips,
round ears showing off diamond earring clips.
The little face looking at me smiled just suddenly.
Today I am happy, I've a funny feeling inside
for today is my birthday and I feel alive.
For how I feel inside reflects on my face,
how wonderful the world would be if there was a smile
on the whole human race.

Charlie-Rose Mansfield (8)
Wincheap Junior GM School

Stars Take Over The Galaxy

Stars, stars whizz through space
they shimmer like gold.
They burn like burning fire.
I see planets spinning around.
Out of the black hole
comes something big.
Can you guess what it is?
We jump far away
as they shimmer past.
They are
Stars, stars, stars.

Sammy-Jo Smith (9)
Wouldham School

THE GLOOMY NIGHT

When the night is dark
The stars have a big spark
In the night the flashing stars
are glowing bright.
The twinkling moon reflects the blinding sun
and the night is beginning to fade away.

Claire Jayne Gregory (9)
Wouldham School

I STARED UP AT THE SKY

When I stared up at the sky
as the day drifts away.
It winks at me,
it smiles at me
and I smile back.
What can it be?

Cally Baldwin (9)
Wouldham School

STARS

Shoots through the sky
Till it comes crashing down on Earth
Amazement from the crowd
Run, run it's on fire!

Stephanie Kingsland (8)
Wouldham School

Cosmic Poem

When the sun goes down
the moon goes up
and when the stars come up with a bump.
They glitter like diamonds,
and Earth is like blue and green.
But the moon is white
and the moon goes down and the stars
and the sun comes up
and the day begins.

Emma Hargreaves (8)
Wouldham School

Cosmic

In the gloomy dark of night
The sparkling stars are shining
Bright as golden candles
The planet that lights our night
Is made of silver cheese
I hope one sparkling night
The shooting candles will return.

Jennifer Stokes (8)
Wouldham School

STAR SOLAR POWER

I live on planet Mars
I come from the sun
I power things on Earth
I worship the sun
What I am is easy . . .

Do you want to guess?

(Solar Power)

Thomas Bennett (8)
Wouldham School

SHOOTING STARS

Shooting stars, shooting stars,
Zooming past planet Mars
With fire burning and
Rockets turning,
The rushing stars spin past the moon,
Forwards, forwards into the gloom.
Shooting stars, shooting stars.

Lauren Young (9)
Wouldham School